NUMBER RIDDLES

FOR

BRIGHT SPARKS

Puzzles and solutions by
Dr Gareth Moore
B.Sc (Hons) M.Phil Ph.D

Illustrations by Jess Bradley
and Adam Linley

Designed and edited by Tall Tree

NUMBER RIDDLES

FOR

BRIGHT SPARKS

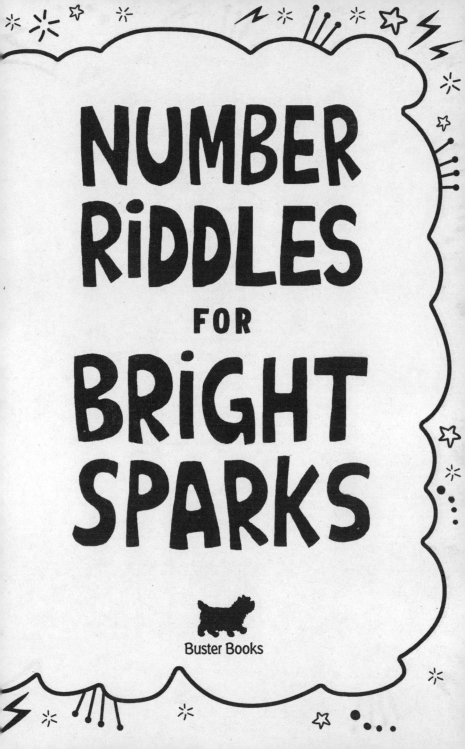

Buster Books

First published in Great Britain in 2022 by Buster Books,
an imprint of Michael O'Mara Books Limited,
9 Lion Yard, Tremadoc Road, London SW4 7NQ

 www.mombooks.com/buster   f Buster Books   🐦 @BusterBooks   @buster_books

Puzzles and solutions © Gareth Moore 2022
Illustrations and layouts © Buster Books 2022

A CIP catalogue record for this book is available
from the British Library.

ISBN: 978-1-78055-783-0

2 4 6 8 10 9 7 5 3 1

Papers used by Buster Books are natural, recyclable products made of wood from
well-managed, FSC®-certified forests and other controlled sources. The manufacturing
processes conform to the environmental regulations of the country of origin.

Printed and bound in April 2022 by CPI Group (UK) Ltd,
108 Beddington Lane, Croydon, CR0 4YY, United Kingdom.

INTRODUCTION

This book is packed with more than 80 amazing number riddles to challenge your brain. Are you ready to tackle them?

The puzzles get harder as the book progresses, so it's best to start at the beginning and work your way through. You'll see a little clock symbol at the bottom of each puzzle. Use this space to record how long each game takes you to complete.

The instructions for each number riddle will tell you how to get started. If you're not sure what to do, read them again in case there is something you've missed. Many of the number riddles also include a finished example that will help you along the way.

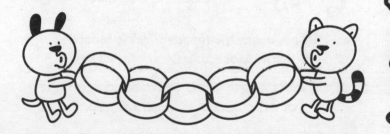

There's plenty of space on the pages to make notes as you go, but if you need more room to work out your answers, use the blank pages at the back of the book.

Use a pencil to fill in your answers, then you can change them if you need to.

If you are still stuck, you could also try asking a grown-up. If you're *really* stuck, have a peek at the answers in the back of the book, and then try and work out how you could have got to that solution yourself.

Good luck and have fun!

Introducing the Number-Riddle Master: Gareth Moore, B.Sc (Hons) M.Phil Ph.D

Dr Gareth Moore is an Ace Puzzler and author of many puzzle and maths books.

He created online brain-training site BrainedUp.com, and runs the online puzzle site PuzzleMix.com. Gareth has a Ph.D from the University of Cambridge, where he taught machines to understand spoken English.

LET THE NUMBER RIDDLES BEGIN!

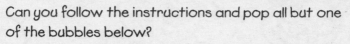

Can you follow the instructions and pop all but one of the bubbles below?

- Pop all bubbles containing numbers in the 3 times table.

- Next, pop all the remaining bubbles containing numbers which are greater than 15.

- Finally, pop all the bubbles that contain even numbers.

What number is in the only remaining bubble?

....

TIME

....

AMAZING AGES

It's Yaz's ninth birthday today. She is chatting to her friends, Jenny, Sam and Miriam, about how old they all are. They notice that:

• Jenny's age is double Miriam's age.

• Miriam is two years younger than Yaz was last week.

• Sam is one year older than Miriam.

How old are Jenny, Sam and Miriam?

Jenny ....

Sam ....

Miriam ....

TIME

....

MONSTER PARTY

There are two types of monster on planet Flink:

• Yellow monsters, which have 3 legs.

• Blue monsters, which have 4 legs.

Today, there is a party for both yellow and blue monsters. There are 4 monsters at the party, and between them all they have 14 legs in total.

How many yellow monsters are at the party, and how many blue monsters?

Yellow monsters ....

Blue monsters ....

TIME

NUMBER DARTS

Can you form each of the given totals by choosing one number from each ring of this dartboard?

For example, you could make a total of 3 by picking 1 from the inner ring and 2 from the outer ring.

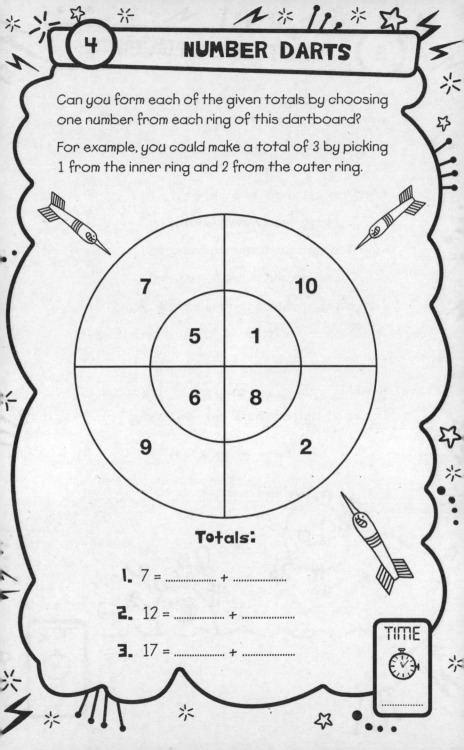

Totals:

1. 7 = ... + ...

2. 12 = ... + ...

3. 17 = ... + ...

TIME

....

Jaz is practising for a swimming competition by swimming lengths of her local swimming pool.

To help with her training, she swims further each day.

- On Monday, she swims 3 lengths.
- On Tuesday, she swims 6 lengths.
- On Wednesday, she swims 9 lengths.
- On Thursday, she swims 12 lengths.

Can you spot the pattern she is following?

1. How many lengths will Jaz swim on Friday?

.... lengths

2. If she continues with the same pattern, how many lengths will she swim on Sunday?

.... lengths

TIME

EQUAL AMOUNTS

Jess and Tom have been making jam together at school, and have been given six jars to put their jam in.

When they finish putting the jam into jars, they have:

- 3 jars that are full of jam.
- 2 jars that are exactly half-full.
- 1 jar that is empty.

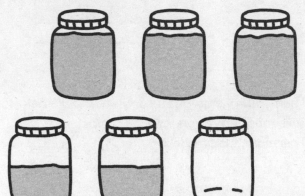

Between them they want to take home all the jam and all the jars, and to make sure they each have exactly the same amount of jam as the other.

How can they pour the jam between the jars so that they both take home exactly the same number of full jars, half-full jars and empty jars?

TIME

You have 8 blocks built in a 2x2x2 tower, so they look like this:

EXAMPLE:

Then you take away the 3 white blocks below, and count how many blocks remain.
There are 5 blocks left:

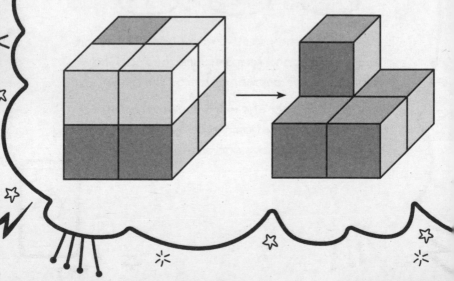

You build three more 2x2x2 block cubes, then take some blocks away from each tower. How many blocks are left in each pile now?

1.

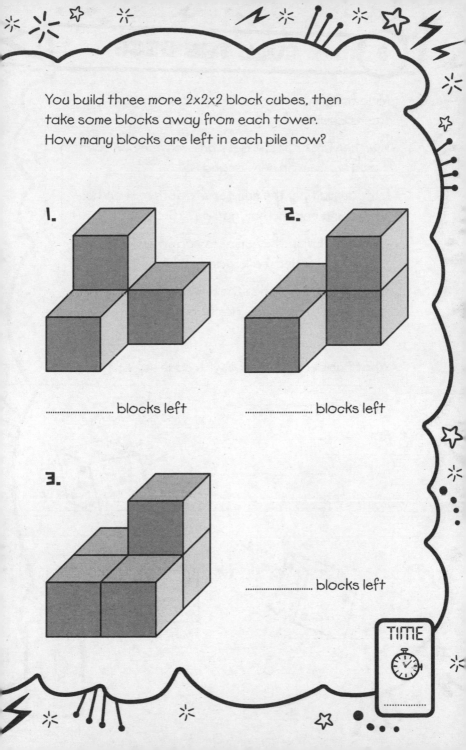

.... blocks left

2.

.... blocks left

3.

.... blocks left

TIME

Mina rolls a dice four times, and notices the following:

- On her first roll she gets an even number, then an odd number on her second roll.

- If you multiply the numbers together from her first and second roll, you get 10.

- If you multiply the numbers together from her third and fourth rolls, you get 12.

- If you add together the numbers from her first and fourth rolls, you get 6.

What number did she roll with each roll of the dice?

Roll 1 = ...

Roll 2 = ...

Roll 3 = ...

Roll 4 = ...

TIME

....

NUMBER LINES

Start by filling in the missing numbers on the number line below:

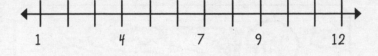

1   4   7   9   12

Now see if you can follow these instructions:

• Start on the number which is **half of 6**.

• Now jump to the number that results from **adding 2**.

• Now jump to the number which is **2 times** this number.

• Now jump to the number that results from **subtracting 3**.

1. Which number have you finished on? ....

2. If you began again at the number you started on, what number would you have to add to get to the number you finished on?

....

TIME

....

All of the sums that are in the same position on these two pictures have the same answer, apart from five. Can you circle all five sums whose answers are different?

Once you have found the five different sum results, can you also find five visual differences between the two pictures?

2x8

20+60

100-9

5+3

11+5

2x2

12-4

5x6

10-5

2x4

20-4

25-25

99+2

14+1

TIME

BRAIN CHAINS

Here are some fun mental arithmetic puzzles to test your number skills.

Begin with the number at the top of each puzzle and apply all of the instructions in turn, from top to bottom. Keep going until you reach the empty box, then write your answer there. To make it extra tricky try to do all of the sums in your head, without writing anything down until each final answer.

In the first puzzle, for example, you would start with 8, then divide by 2 (to make 4), then add 20 (to make 24) and so on.

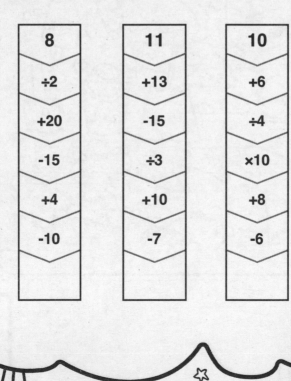

8	11	10
÷2	+13	+6
+20	-15	÷4
-15	÷3	×10
+4	+10	+8
-10	-7	-6

TIME

PENCIL PROBLEM

Kim's pencil case has five red and five blue pencils in it, and no other colours.

She wants to take out two pencils of the same colour, but instead of looking inside it to pick them out she decides to play a game:

- Kim will close her eyes and take a pencil out without looking at it.

- Still without looking, she will carry on removing pencils one-by-one until she is certain that she will have taken out at least two pencils that are the same colour.

What is the fewest number of pencils Kim needs to take out, given that she isn't looking at them, to be sure of having at least two of the same colour?

A:

TIME

MYSTERY NUMBERS

1. Emma is thinking of a number between 1 and 10. Can you use the following clues to work out which number it is?
- It's an odd number.
- It's higher than five.
- It's not in the 3 times table.

What is the number?

....

2. Emma is now thinking of a different number between 1 and 10.
- It's lower than the previous number she thought of.
- It's in the 3 times table.
- It's an even number.

What is her new number?

....

TIME

....

ORANGE SEGMENTS

Jenny has an orange, which she has peeled and split into eight segments so she can eat it slowly.

It takes exactly one minute for her to eat one segment of orange. Then, once she has eaten a segment, she waits exactly five minutes before she eats another segment.

How long will it take Jenny to eat the whole orange, from when she starts eating the first segment to when she finishes eating the last segment?

....

TIME

....

Can you work out which of the following numbers is the odd one out, and say why?

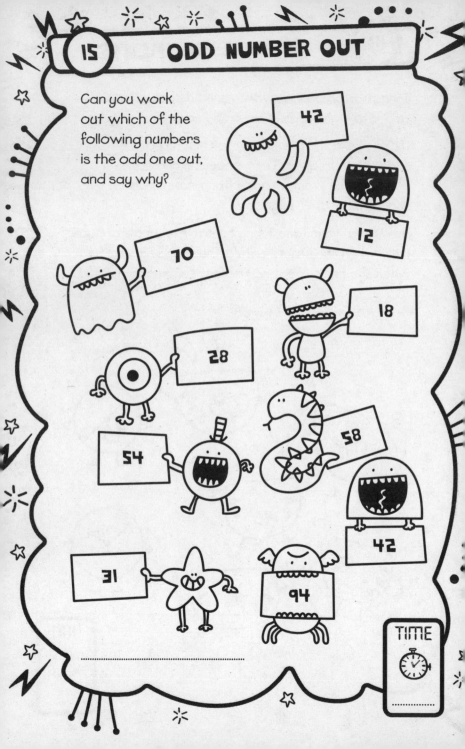

42

12

70

18

28

58

54

42

31

94

TIME

....

SUMS MATCH

Join all except one of these balloons into pairs, so that both balloons in each pair are equal to the same number. Which balloon is left over?

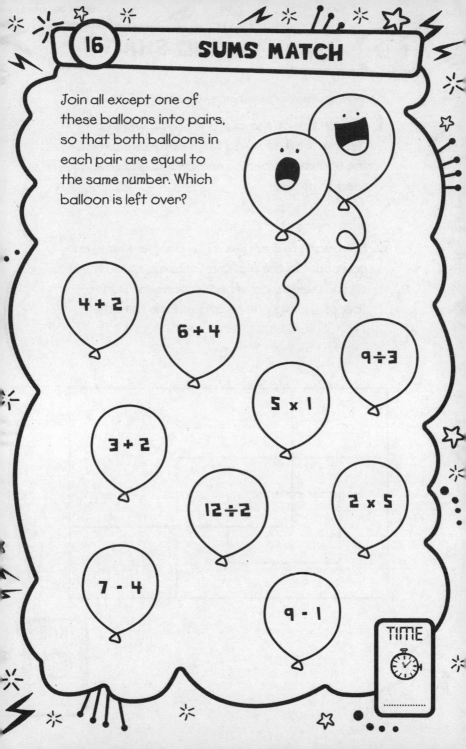

4 + 2

6 + 4

9 ÷ 3

5 x 1

3 + 2

12 ÷ 2

2 x 5

7 - 4

9 - 1

TIME

It's time to test your shape-counting skills.

1. Take a look at this picture. If you were to redraw it by drawing only rectangles, what is the fewest number of rectangles you would need to draw?

   ....

2. How many rectangles of all different sizes can you count in the picture, including those formed by the overlap of other rectangles? Don't forget the big one all around the outside!

   ....

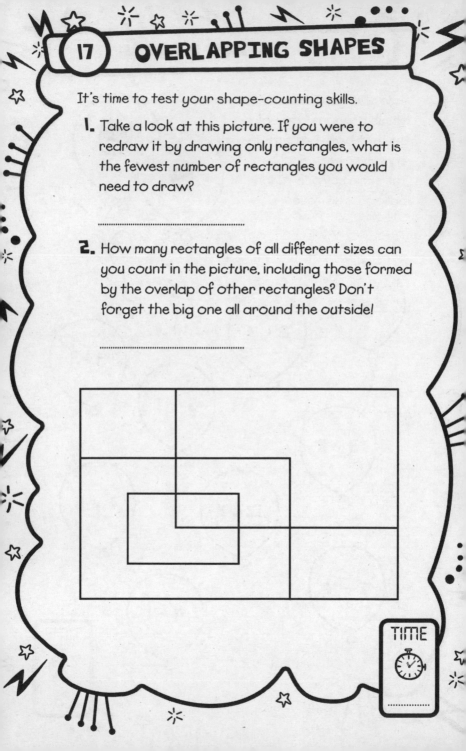

TIME

....

MARSHMALLOW WINNERS

Sara, Nat and Evan have all just taken part in a running race, and have won prizes for being the three fastest runners. Each prize is a bag of marshmallows.

• Sara wins a bag of three marshmallows.

• The person in second place gets half as many marshmallows as the winner.

• The number of marshmallows won by Evan is a third of the number won by the winner.

• Nat wins six marshmallows.

Can you use the information to fill out the table to show who finished first, second and third, and what their prizes were?

Person	Finishing position	Number of marshmallows

Can you draw lines to join all of these animals into pairs, so that each animal has a line connecting to one other animal?

Animals should be paired if the number on one shirt is **twice** (2x) the value of the other. For example, the animal wearing the '5' shirt should be paired with the animal wearing the '10' shirt, since 5 x 2 = 10.

TIME

BIRTHDAY BALLOONS

Janice works in a balloon shop. Customers come into the shop, each wanting balloons to celebrate various birthdays.

The shop only sells balloons with the following numbers on:

4   6   8   12   15

For each customer, which numbered balloons should Janice sell to them so that the balloons add up to the exact age required? Janice can't sell any number more than once to the same person.

1. Age 16 =

◯ + ◯

2. Age 21 =

◯ + ◯

3. Age 24 =

◯ + ◯ + ◯

4. Age 35 =

◯ + ◯ + ◯

TIME

NUMBER PYRAMIDS

Fill in all of the empty squares to complete each of these number pyramids. Every square must contain a number equal to the result of adding the two squares directly beneath it.

In this example, notice how the 8 is equal to the sum of the two squares beneath, the 6 and the 2.

EXAMPLE:

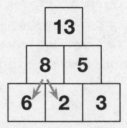

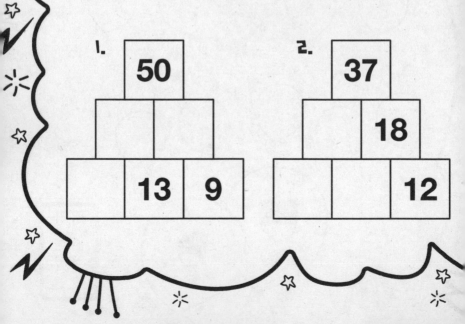

3.

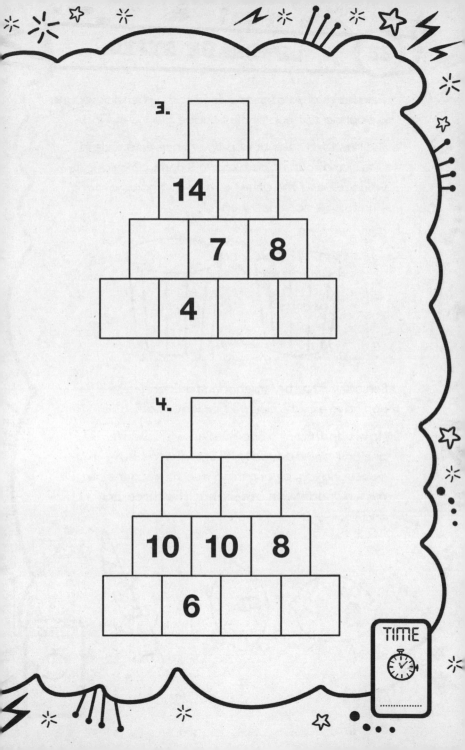

14

7 8

4

4.

10 10 8

6

TIME

LEMONADE STAND

Julia has set up a lemonade stand by her house, and is pouring out cups of lemonade from a big jug.

She has two sizes of cup to sell her lemonade in. One size of cup holds exactly 3 units of lemonade when full, and the other size of cup holds exactly 4 units of lemonade when full.

3 units   4 units

Ben comes to the lemonade stand and asks if he can have exactly one unit of lemonade.

How can Julia fill a cup for Ben with *exactly* one unit of lemonade in it? She doesn't have a measuring jug, or anything else to measure out the lemonade with other than the three-unit and four-unit cups.

TIME

TIME FLIES

See if you can work out what time each of the following clocks would show, if changed as shown.

1. `04:00pm` + 3 hours = `88:88am`

2. `02:30pm` + 6 hours = `88:88am`

3. `05:00am` + 12 hours = `88:88am`

4. `07:30am` − 3 hours = `88:88am`

5. `09:00am` + 8 hours = `88:88am`

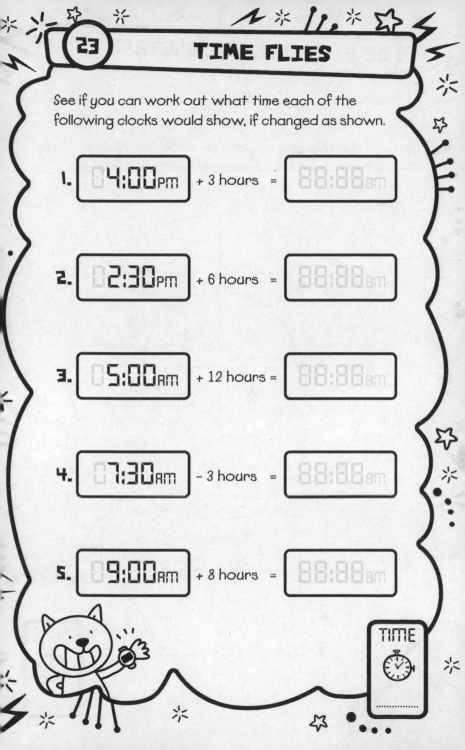

TIME

DART GAME

Can you form each of the given totals by choosing one number from each ring of this dartboard?

For example, you could make a total of 10 by picking 4 from the inner ring and 6 from the outer ring.

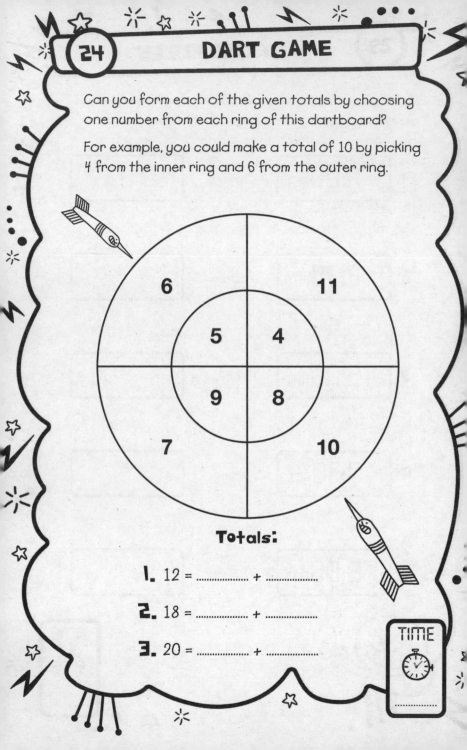

6   11

5   4

9   8

7   10

Totals:

1. 12 = ... + ...

2. 18 = ... + ...

3. 20 = ... + ...

TIME

....

MAGIC BEANS

Jack is about to leave home to go to the market, where everyone pays in magic beans. He wants to buy something at the market which costs exactly two magic beans.

On his way to the market, Jack has to pass over three bridges. Each bridge has a guard, who charges exactly half the number of magic beans you have. Once you have paid the guard and crossed the bridge, they give you back one magic bean.

Jack needs to arrive at the market with exactly two magic beans. What is the lowest number of magic beans that Jack can leave home with?

TIME

SHELL COUNT

Jon is on holiday, and each day he collects a different number of shells from the beach.

- On Monday, he collects 2 shells.
- On Tuesday, he collects 3 shells.
- On Wednesday, he collects 5 shells.
- On Thursday, he collects 8 shells.
- On Friday, he collects 12 shells.

Can you spot the pattern he is following?

1. How many shells will Jon collect on Saturday?

....

2. If he continues with the same pattern, how many shells would he collect on Sunday?

....

TIME

....

SALES PRICE

Each of the items below has a price tag, and they are all on sale.

After the discounts, how much money would you need to buy all 5 items?

 Take $\frac{1}{2}$ off the marked price.

 Take $\frac{1}{4}$ off the marked price.

 Take $\frac{1}{3}$ off the marked price.

 Take $\frac{3}{4}$ off the marked price.

 Take $\frac{1}{2}$ off the marked price.

To buy all the items, you would need to spend:

....

TIME

....

ELIMINATION GAME

Can you eliminate all of the numbers in this grid until only one remains?

4	21	3	16
10	7	13	17
20	9	15	12
8	19	11	6

- Shade in all the numbers in the 4 times table.
- Next, shade in all the numbers in the 3 times table.
- Finally, shade in all the numbers with two digits.

Which is the only number left?

....

TIME

....

JOIN THE HALVES

Can you draw lines to join each number in a bubble to its matching sum? For example, a number 7 could be joined to a sum of 3+4, since 3+4 = 7.

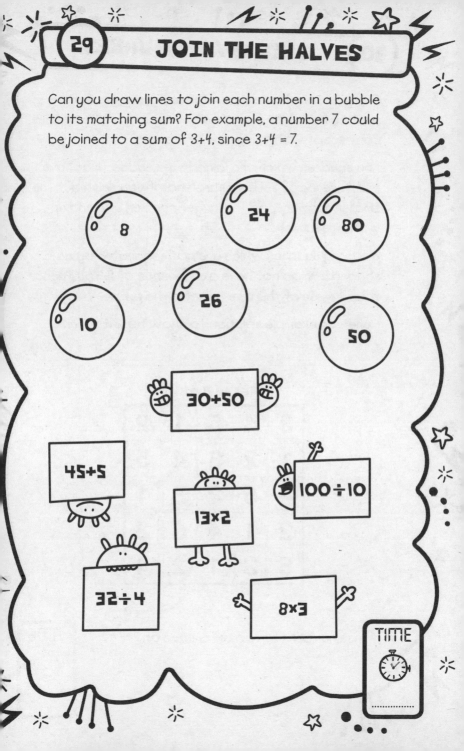

8

24

80

10

26

50

30+50

45+5

13×2

100÷10

32÷4

8×3

TIME

....

Can you complete each of these puzzles by writing a number from 1 to 5 in every empty square? No number can repeat within any row or column.

Any squares which are joined by a shaded bar have a *difference* of 2. This means that if you subtract the smaller number from the larger number, you end up with a result of 2.

Also, any squares which are *not* separated by a shaded bar **do not have a difference of 2**. You'll need to make use of this rule to solve the puzzle.

Here's an example solution to show how it works:

EXAMPLE:

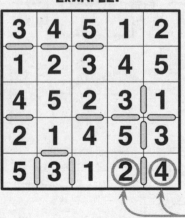

These numbers have a difference of 2.

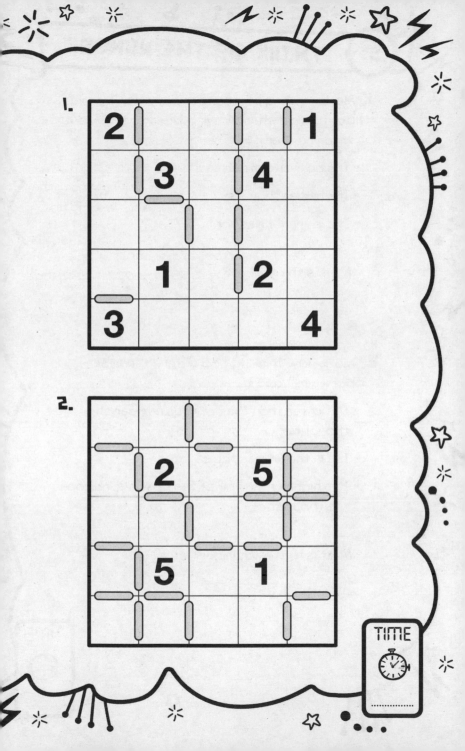

THINK OF THE NUMBER

1. Mai is thinking of a number between 1 and 15. Can you use the following clues to work out which number it is?

- It's an even number.

- It's higher than six.

- It's in the 3 times table.

What is the number?

....

2. Mai is now thinking of a different number between 1 and 15.

- It's lower than the previous number she thought of.

- It's in the 5 times table.

- It is higher than half of the previous number she thought of.

What is her new number?

....

TIME

....

TOP TO BOTTOM

Test your mental arithmetic with these puzzles!

Begin with the number at the top of each puzzle and apply all of the instructions in turn, from top to bottom. Keep going until you reach the empty box, then write your answer there. To make it extra tricky try to do all of the sums in your head, without writing anything down until each final answer.

In the first puzzle, for example, you would start with 10, then multiply by 5 (to make 50), then add 1 (to make 51) and so on.

10	20	15
×5	+17	-8
+1	-3	×5
÷3	×2	+17
×2	-7	÷4
-7	+16	+8

TIME

Amos and Zoe are brother and sister. They are twins, so they are in the same class at school.

At school, their teacher asks them if they have any more brothers and sisters in their family.

They both say yes.

Amos says, 'I have the same number of sisters as brothers.'

Zoe says, 'I have twice as many brothers as sisters.'

How many brothers and how many sisters are there in total, in Amos and Zoe's family?

....

TIME

PIZZA PROBLEMS

Doug, Nic and Fai are all sharing a pizza, which they have cut into 12 identical pieces.

- Doug eats 4 slices of pizza.
- Fai eats a quarter of the number of slices that Doug eats.
- Nic eats a quarter of the whole pizza.

See if you can answer these questions:

1. How many pieces of pizza did each person eat?

Doug ....

Fai ....

Nic ....

2. How many slices are left over?

....

3. What fraction of the original pizza has been eaten?

....

TIME

....

PYRAMID POWER

Fill in all of the empty squares to complete each of these number pyramids. Every square must contain a number equal to the result of adding the two squares directly beneath it.

In this example, notice how the 8 is equal to the sum of the two squares beneath, the 6 and 2.

EXAMPLE:

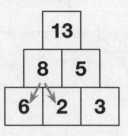

```
    13
   8   5
  6   2   3
```

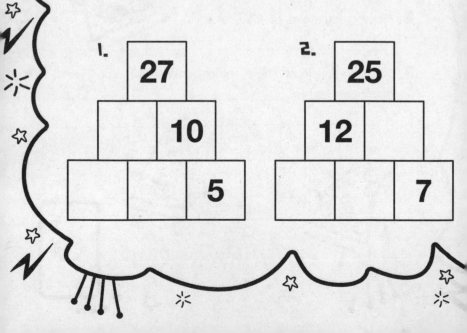

1.
```
    27
      10
          5
```

2.
```
    25
   12
          7
```

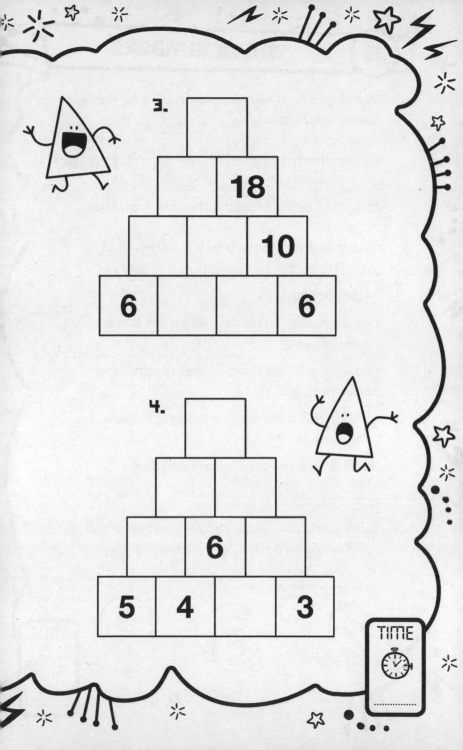

TRAIN NUMBERS

Start by filling in the missing numbers on the ladder number line below:

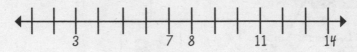

3   7 8   11   14

Now see if you can follow these instructions:

- Start on the number which is **a third of 12**.

- Now jump to the number that results from **subtracting 3**.

- Now jump to the number which is **9 times** this number.

- Now jump to the number that results from **subtracting 2**.

- Now jump to the number which is **2 times** this number.

1. Which number have you finished at?

....

2. What number would you have to add to the starting number to get to the finishing number?

....

TIME

IDENTICAL PAIRS

Can you join the robots into pairs whose sums result in the same value?

Some of the sums might be too hard for you to work out, but you can use your number skills to decide which **must** form into pairs. For example, if exactly two of the sums will result in much bigger numbers than all of the others, they must form a pair.

1×5

30×2

55×2

1000×10

35÷5

100×100

14÷2

20÷4

80-20

100+10

TIME
....

Your sister is making a long paper chain to decorate your hall. Every day this week she has been getting faster and faster at connecting the loops of paper, and each day she has doubled the length of her paper chain.

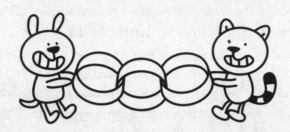

On the sixth day, your sister's paper chain becomes long enough to stretch across the whole length of your hall.

How many days did it take your sister to make her chain long enough to stretch across **half** the length of the hall?

....

TIME

....

PARTY TIME

Sinead works in a party shop. Customers come into the shop, each wanting balloons to celebrate various birthdays.

The shop only sells balloons with the following numbers on:

5   7   10   13   14

Which numbered balloons should Sinead sell to each customer so that the balloons add up to the exact age required? Sinead can't sell any number more than once to the same person.

1. Age 15 =

◯ + ◯

2. Age 20 =

◯ + ◯

3. Age 30 =

◯ + ◯ + ◯

4. Age 36 =

◯ + ◯ + ◯

TIME

....

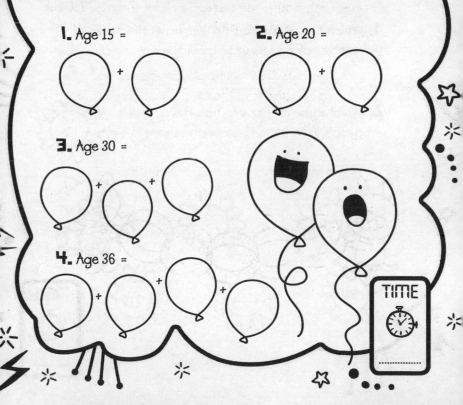

Liam has arranged some flowers in a vase, so that it now has two tulips, three poppies, two lilies and six irises in it.

Liam notices that the flowers in the vase of the same type happen to have the same number of petals:

- The irises have 5 petals each.
- The poppies have 6 petals each.
- The lilies have 7 petals each.
- The tulips have 9 petals each.

1. Which two types of flower have the same number of petals in total in the arrangement?

....

2. Which type of flower has the most petals in total in the arrangement?

....

TIME

....

GRAPE PROBLEM

Luci and her brother Dan are sharing a bunch of grapes, and decide they don't want to eat them all at once. Instead, they will eat just a few each day.

- On the first day, Luci eats 1 grape and Dan eats 3.

- On the second day, Luci eats 2 grapes and Dan eats 5.

- On the third day, Luci eats 4 grapes and Dan eats 7.

- On the fourth day, Luci eats 8 grapes and Dan eats 9.

Can you spot the pattern that Luci is using, and the pattern that Dan is using?

If they carry on using the same patterns, which one of these statements will be true?

a. On the fifth day, Luci will eat 12 grapes and Dan will eat 13.

b. On the fifth day, Luci will eat 24 grapes and Dan will eat 11.

c. On the fifth day, Luci will eat 32 grapes and Dan will eat 15.

d. On the fifth day, Luci will eat 16 grapes and Dan will eat 11.

TIME

....

ADD THEM UP

Can you form each of the given totals by choosing one number from each ring of this dartboard?

For example, you could make a total of 7 by picking 2 from the inner ring, 4 from the centre ring and 1 from the outer ring.

10   1

5   11

2   9

3   12

4   13

7   8

Totals:

1. 9 = ... + ... + ...

2. 28 = ... + ... + ...

3. 35 = ... + ... + ...

TIME

....

Eddie is having a birthday party, and has invited 15 people from school. He wants to make each of these 15 people a party hat, plus one for himself, so that they can all wear matching hats at the party.

If Eddie makes four hats each day until the day of the party, and starts today, then he will make the last four hats on the day of the party.

The party is on the 11th April.

1. What day is it today?

....

2. If Eddie only manages to make two hats a day, starting today, then on what day will he have made half of the hats he needs?

....

TIME

HOW MANY SHAPES?

It's time to test your shape-counting skills again.

1. Take a look at this picture. If you were to redraw it by drawing only rectangles, what is the fewest number of rectangles you would need to draw?

....

2. How many rectangles of all different sizes can you count in the picture, including those formed by the overlap of other rectangles? Don't forget the big one all around the outside!

....

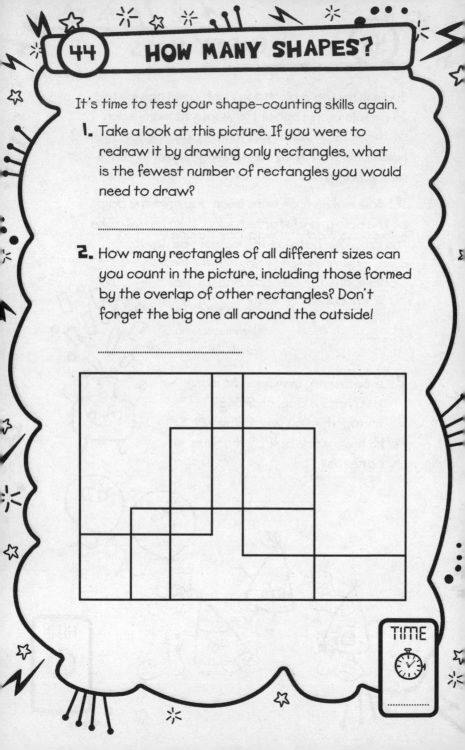

TIME

SOCK SUMS

Daisy and Ron have a bag containing four pairs of socks: two red pairs and two yellow pairs. Each of these pairs of socks is balled up so that the two socks in each pair stay together.

They decide to play a game:

- Daisy will close her eyes and take each balled pair of socks from the bag, one by one.

- Without looking, she will create two piles of socks: one for her, and one for Ron.

- When all the socks have been pulled out of the bag, each pile should have exactly the same number of red socks and yellow socks as the other pile.

How can Daisy do this, given that she has her eyes closed and can't see the colour of each ball of socks she is pulling out?

....

....

....

TIME

Julia is running a lemonade stand by her house, with lots of lemonade to sell from a big jug.

She has two sizes of cup to sell her lemonade in. One size of cup holds exactly three units of lemonade when full, and the other size of cup holds exactly four units of lemonade when full.

3 units   4 units

Anna comes to the lemonade stand and asks if she can have exactly two units of lemonade.

How can Julia fill a cup for Anna with exactly two units of lemonade in it? She doesn't have a measuring jug, or anything else to measure out the lemonade with other than the three-unit and four-unit cups. She also doesn't want to throw away any lemonade, or pour it back into the jug once she's poured it into a cup.

TIME

ROBOT FRIENDS

Can you draw lines to join all of these robots into pairs, so each robot has a line connecting it to one other robot?

Robots should be paired if the number on one shirt is **four** times (4x) the value of the other. For example, the robot wearing the '5' shirt should be paired with the robot wearing the '20' shirt, since 5 x 4 = 20.

28

3

12

5

7

40

8

10

20

2

9

36

TIME

You have 18 blocks built into a 3x2x3 tower, so they look like this:

EXAMPLE:

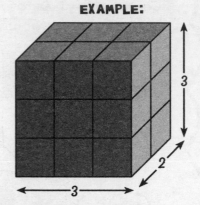

You build three more identical block towers, then take some blocks away from each tower. How many blocks are left in each pile now?

I.

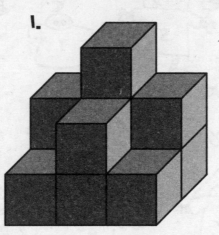

.... blocks left

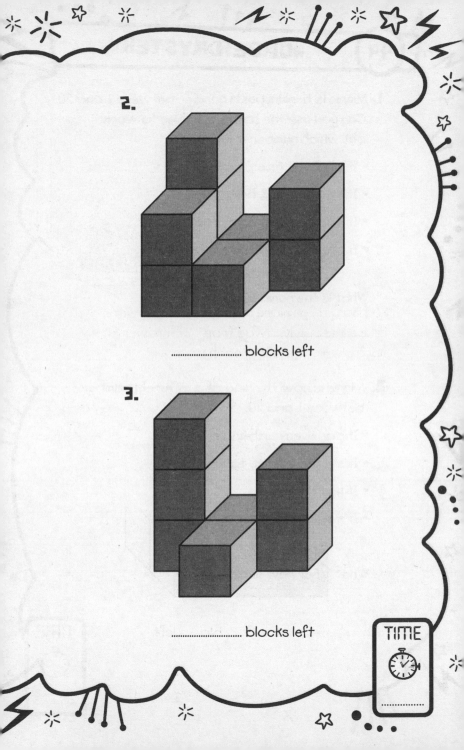

2.

.... blocks left

3.

.... blocks left

TIME

....

NUMBER MYSTERY

1. Minnie is thinking of a number between 1 and 20. Can you use the following clues to work out which number it is?

- It's in the 4 times table.
- It's not in the 3 times table.
- It's not in the 5 times table.
- It's higher than ten.

What is the number?

....

2. Minnie is now thinking of a different number between 1 and 20.

- It's an even number.
- It's in the 3 times table.
- It has two digits.
- It's not in the 4 times table.

What is her new number?

....

TIME

....

CLOCK PUZZLE

Work out what time each of the following clocks would show, if changed as shown, and then draw this time on the associated clock face.

1. 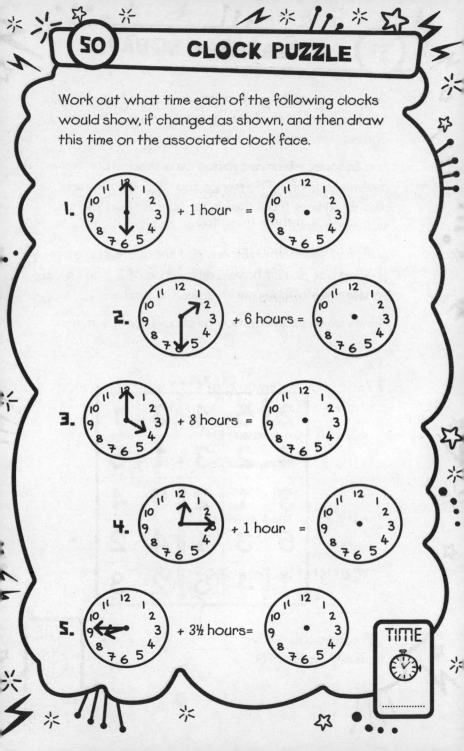 + 1 hour =

2. + 6 hours =

3. + 8 hours =

4. + 1 hour =

5. + 3½ hours=

TIME

....

Can you complete each of these puzzles by writing a number from 1 to 5 in every empty square? No number can repeat within any row or column.

Any squares which are joined by a shaded bar have a *difference* of 3. This means that if you subtract the smaller number from the larger number, you end up with a result of 3.

Also, any squares which are *not* separated by a shaded bar **do not have a difference of 3.** You'll need to make use of this rule to solve the puzzle.

Here's an example solution to show how it works:

EXAMPLE:

These numbers have
a difference of 3.

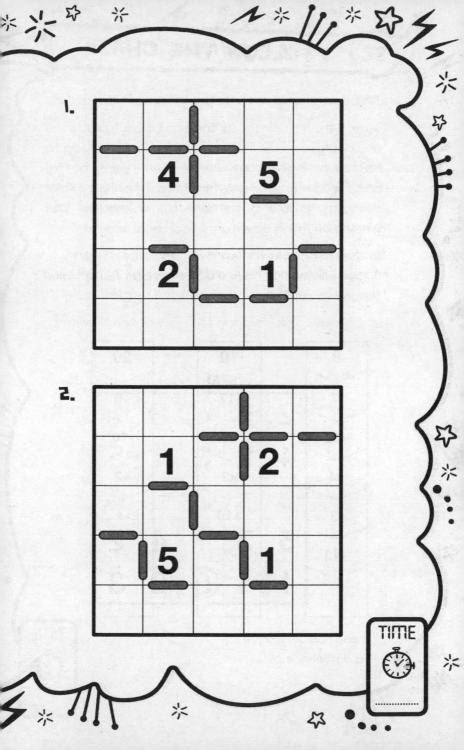

1.

2.

TIME

FOLLOW THE CHAIN

Test your mental arithmetic with these puzzles!

Begin with the number at the top of each puzzle and apply all of the instructions in turn, from top to bottom. Keep going until you reach the empty bottom box, then write your answer there. To make it extra tricky, try to do all of the sums in your head, without writing anything down until each final answer.

In the first puzzle, for example, you would start with 9, then subtract 7 (to make 2), then add 12 (to make 14) and so on.

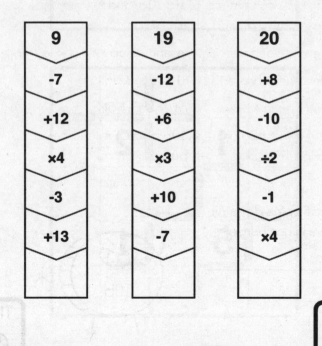

9	19	20
-7	-12	+8
+12	+6	-10
×4	×3	÷2
-3	+10	-1
+13	-7	×4

TIME

SWEET SUMS

Ali lives in Bafan, where the currency is the borit. This is usually shortened to '**b**', so it's easier to write.

There are four different values of borit coin – 1b, 2b, 5b and 10b.

1b   2b   5b   10b

Ali wants to buy a bag of sweets from a vending machine. Each bag of sweets costs 10b, and the machine doesn't give any change.

When Ali opens her purse, she discovers three things:

• Her purse has exactly 13b inside it.

• She doesn't have any of the 1b coins.

• She can't pay for the 10b bag of sweets exactly, using the coins in her purse.

What coins does Ali have in her purse?

....

10b

TIME

....

Fill in all of the empty squares to complete each of these number pyramids. Every square must contain a number equal to the result of adding the two squares directly beneath it.

In this example, notice how the 6 is equal to the sum of the two squares beneath, the 1 and 5.

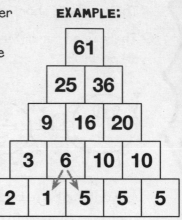

EXAMPLE:

I.

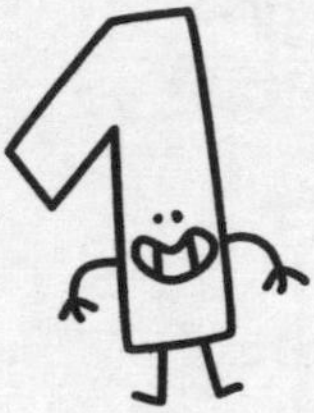

2.

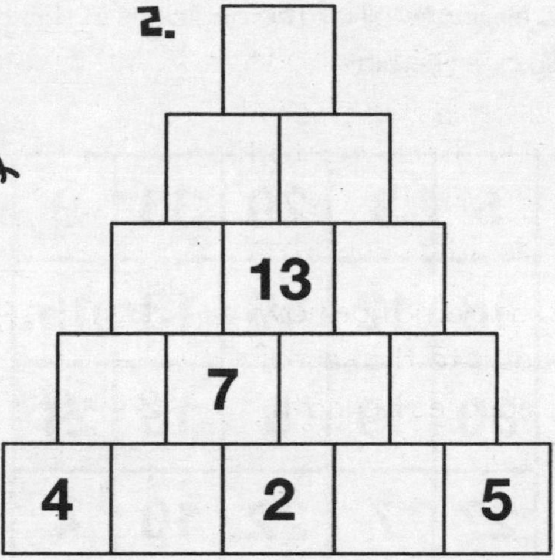
13
7
4 2 5

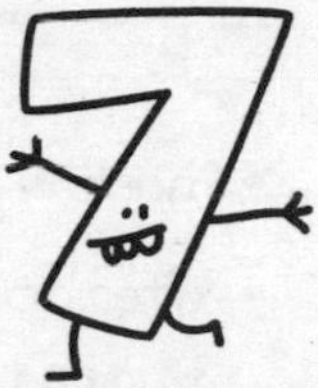

3.

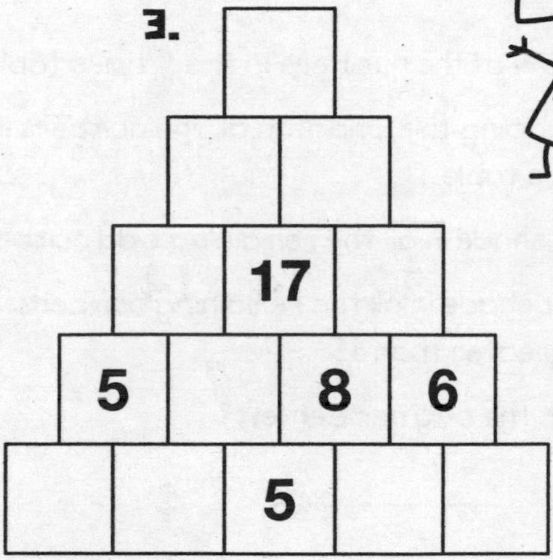
17
5 8 6
5

TIME

SHADY NUMBERS

Can you eliminate all of the numbers in this grid until only one remains?

5	3	20	33	9
18	12	40	13	15
30	19	6	16	21
27	7	22	10	4
17	25	1	11	35

- Shade in all the numbers in the 5 times table.

- After doing this, shade in all the numbers in the 3 times table.

- Then, shade in all the remaining odd numbers.

- Finally, shade in all the remaining numbers which are greater than 15.

Which is the only number left?

....

TIME

....

Each of the items below has a price tag, and they are all on sale.

After the discounts, which item is the cheapest and which item is the most expensive?

Cheapest...

Most expensive ....

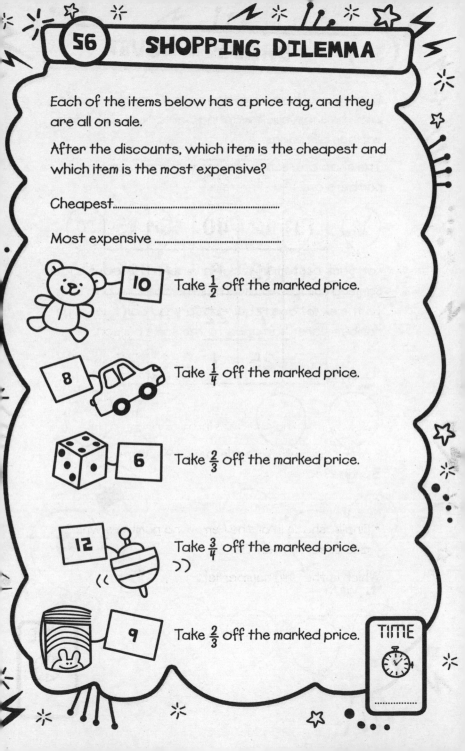

10   Take $\frac{1}{2}$ off the marked price.

8   Take $\frac{1}{4}$ off the marked price.

6   Take $\frac{2}{3}$ off the marked price.

12   Take $\frac{3}{4}$ off the marked price.

9   Take $\frac{2}{3}$ off the marked price.

TIME

BALLOON COUNT

Sanjeed works in a balloon shop. Customers come into the shop, each wanting balloons to celebrate various birthdays.

The shop only sells balloons with the following numbers on:

(12)   (13)   (18)   (19)   (20)

For each customer, which numbered balloons should Sanjeed sell to them so that the balloons add up to the exact age required? Sanjeed can't sell any number more than once to the same person.

1. Age 25 =

◯ + ◯

2. Age 33 =

◯ + ◯

3. Age 49 =

◯ + ◯ + ◯

4. Age 64 =

◯ + ◯ + ◯ + ◯

TIME

....

SUM NUMBERS

Can you draw lines to join each number in a cloud to its matching sum? For example, a number 8 could be joined to a sum of 2+6, since 2+6 = 8.

7

10

30

104

60

1000

100×10

50 ÷ 5

28 ÷ 4

20+40

15×2

14+90

TIME

....

SOCK DRAWER PROBLEM

Stephen's socks all have holes in them. He wants to mend them one by one, then put each mended sock into his drawer.

Each day, he mends twice the number of socks that he mended the day before:

- On Monday, he mends one sock.
- On Tuesday, he mends two socks.
- On Wednesday, he mends four socks.

1. Assuming he carries on with the same pattern, which will be the first day of the week that Stephen mends over 20 socks in a single day?

....

2. Stephen's sock drawer was empty before he began repairing the socks. On what day of the week will Stephen first have more than 50 socks in his drawer?

....

TIME

....

HOLIDAY TIME

Ava and Sophie both decide to paint pictures during the school holidays. Each week, they paint fewer pictures than the week before because they don't want to run out of paint before the end of the holidays.

- In the first week of the holidays, Ava paints 50 pictures and Sophie paints 81 pictures.

- In the second week of the holidays, Ava paints 39 pictures and Sophie paints 27 pictures.

- In the third week of the holidays, Ava paints 28 pictures and Sophie paints 9 pictures.

- In the fourth week of the holidays, Ava paints 17 pictures and Sophie paints 3 pictures.

Can you spot the pattern that Ava is using, and the pattern that Sophie is using?

If they carry on using the same patterns, which of these statements will be true?

a. In the fifth week of the holidays, Ava will paint 6 pictures and Sophie will paint 1 picture.

b. In the fifth week of the holidays, Ava will paint 10 pictures and Sophie will paint 2 pictures.

c. In the fifth week of the holidays, Ava will paint 15 pictures and Sophie will paint 2 pictures.

TIME

Rudy is building a really big pyramid out of lots of wooden blocks.

Each of the layers of his pyramid has a different number of blocks in it:

- He starts with the bottom layer, which he builds with 48 blocks.

- He adds a second layer on top of this, which has 42 blocks in total.

- *Rudy* keeps adding layers. Each extra layer *Rudy* builds has 6 fewer blocks than the layer just beneath it.

- When *Rudy* has finished, the top layer of the pyramid has 6 blocks on it.

1. How many layers does *Rudy*'s pyramid have in total?

   ....

2. How many blocks are there in total in the top three layers of *Rudy*'s pyramid?

   ....

TIME

....

DARTBOARD PUZZLE

Can you form each of the given totals by choosing one number from each ring of this dartboard?

For example, you could make a total of 14 by picking 1 from the inner ring, 8 from the centre ring and 5 from the outer ring.

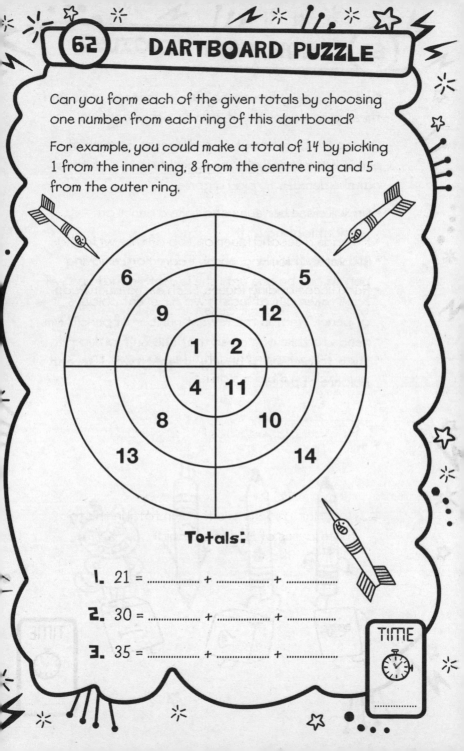

Totals:

1. 21 = ... + ... + ...

2. 30 = ... + ... + ...

3. 35 = ... + ... + ...

TIME

....

Kim's pencil case has three purple, three orange and three yellow pencils in it, and no other colours.

She wants to take out two different colours of pencil, but instead of looking inside it to pick them out she decides to play a game:

- Kim will close her eyes and take a pencil out without looking at it.

- Still without looking, she will carry on removing pencils one by one until she is certain that she will have taken out at least two different colours of pencil. What is the fewest number of pencils Kim needs to take out, given that she isn't looking at them, to be sure of having at least two different colours of pencil?

TIME

BAG OF SWEETS

Gem, Han and Izzi are sharing a bag of sweets. It has 24 sweets in it.

All of the sweets are pink, yellow or red.

- Nine of the sweets are yellow.
- Half of the sweets are pink.
- All the other sweets are red.

See if you can answer these questions:

1. How many of each colour of sweet are there?

Yellow ....

Pink ....

Red ....

2. How many pink sweets would each person get if they were all shared out equally?

....

3. Is it possible to share all the sweets out so that everyone gets the same number of sweets of each colour?

....

TIME

....

You have spent the weekend baking, and have made the following items:

- 9 brownies
- 12 banana muffins
- 20 chocolate-chip cookies
- 24 cupcakes

You want to share these out among 6 people, so that everyone has the same amount of each treat. You don't want to cut any of them up, so you will keep anything left over for yourself.

1. How many items will each of the 6 people end up with?

....

2. If you eat 4 of the leftover items, how many leftover items will remain?

....

TIME

....

WHAT IS LEFT?

Can you eliminate all of the numbers in this grid until only one remains?

8	5	48	26	20
21	25	6	22	12
56	10	4	16	27
24	2	9	18	15
35	40	31	30	32

- Shade in all the numbers in the 8 times table.

- Next, shade in all the numbers in the 5 times table.

- Then, shade in all the remaining numbers which are greater than 20.

- Finally, shade in all the remaining even numbers.

Which is the only number left?

....

TIME

....

There is an object in Rob's classroom which has some numbers written on it.

Looking at this object, Rob notices that:

- If you start with 7, and add 10, you get 5.
- If you start with 9, and add 4, you get 1.
- If you start with 11, and add 5, you get 4.

What object is Rob looking at?

....

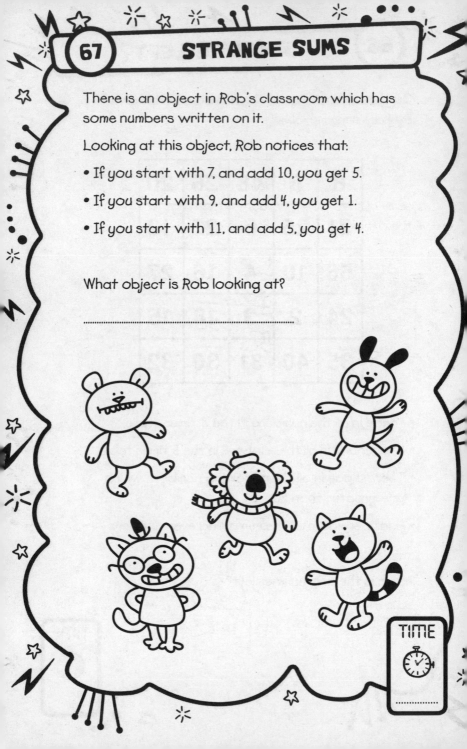

TIME

....

SUM PAIRS

Can you draw lines to join these sums into pairs, so that each pair is equal to the same value?

Some of the sums might be too hard for you to work out, but you can use your number skills to decide which **must** form into pairs. For example, if two of the sums clearly result in much bigger numbers than all of the others, they must form a pair.

3×6

1000×1

9×2

300-98

40-6

250×4

36÷4

17+17

18÷2

101×2

TIME

....

Fill in all of the empty squares to complete each of these number pyramids. Every square must contain a number equal to the result of **multiplying** the two squares directly beneath it.

In this example, notice how the 20 is equal to the squares below, the 5 and the 4, **multiplied** by each other.

EXAMPLE:

240

20	12

5	4	3

I.

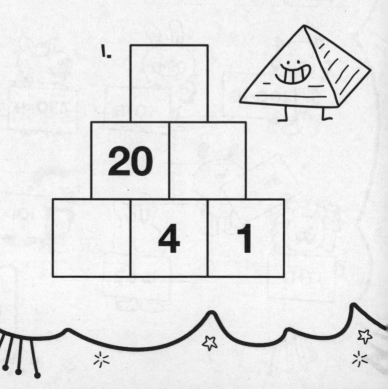

20	

	4	1

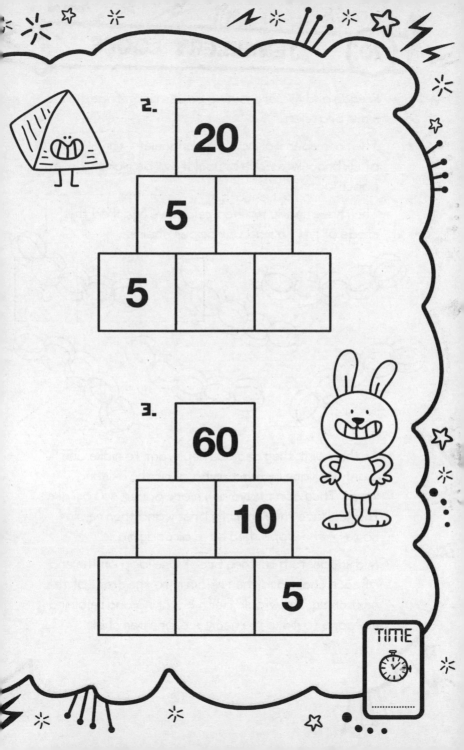

2.

	20	
5		
5		

3.

	60	
	10	
		5

TIME

Freddy and Mia are joining paper rings together to make bracelets.

They are each making three bracelets, for a total of six bracelets. Each bracelet will be made of five paper loops.

They have nearly finished, and have reached the stage of having made six paper chains.

At this point, they decide they want to make one giant necklace instead, using all of the existing loops. They don't have any more paper, so to make the necklace they need to break and then rejoin some of the loops they have already made.

Mia suggests that they break one loop on the end of each chain, and then rejoin it to the start of the next chain. This would mean breaking and rejoining **six** loops to make the necklace, one per chain.

Freddy then suggests a different method, which would mean they only need to break and rejoin **five** loops to make the necklace. His suggestion will still use all of the loops in the necklace.

How can Freddy do this?

....

....

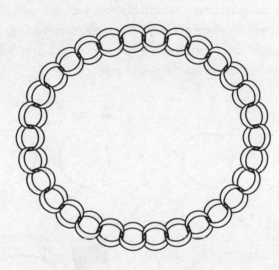

TIME

....

FANCY DRESS QUIZ

Seeta works in a fancy dress shop. Customers sometimes come into the shop, each wanting balloons to celebrate various birthdays.

The shop only sells balloons with the following numbers on:

6   8   9   14   15

For each customer, which numbered balloons should Seeta sell to them so that the balloons add up to the exact age required? Seeta can't sell any number more than once to the same person.

1. Age 17 =

◯ + ◯

2. Age 21 =

◯ + ◯

3. Age 28 =

◯ + ◯ + ◯

4. Age 35 =

◯ + ◯ + ◯

TIME

....

Tess and Scott are looking at a large wall calendar, which shows an entire year from January to December all at once.

1. Tess notices that there is only one month which starts on a Monday and ends on a Sunday. Which month is it?

....

2. Scott notices that a long holiday of exactly 62 days has been marked on the calendar. The holiday lasts for exactly two months, starting on the 1st of one month. Which two months does the holiday cover?

....

TIME

SPONSORED WALK

Violet is going on a sponsored walk to raise money for charity. She has asked her Aunt Kathleen and her Aunt Vicki for donations.

- Aunt Kathleen agrees to sponsor her £12 in total for the first 5 miles she walks, then £4 for each mile she walks after that.

- Aunt Vicki agrees to sponsor her £10 in total for the first 2 miles, then £3 for each mile she walks after that.

If Violet walks 10 miles in total, which aunt will end up donating the most money to charity?

....

TIME

FIND THE NUMBER

1. Moe is thinking of a number between 1 and 25. Can you use the following clues to work out which number it is?

- It's an odd number.

- It has two digits.

- It's in the 3 times table.

- It's not in the 5 times table.

What is the number?

....

2. Moe is now thinking of a different number between 1 and 25.

- It's less than half of the previous number he thought of.

- It's in the 2 times table.

- It's also in the 3 times table.

What is his new number?

....

TIME

....

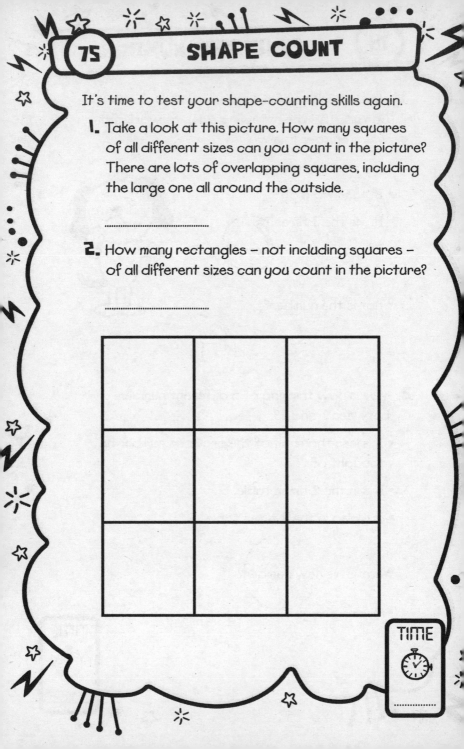

It's time to test your shape-counting skills again.

1. Take a look at this picture. How many squares of all different sizes can you count in the picture? There are lots of overlapping squares, including the large one all around the outside.

....

2. How many rectangles – not including squares – of all different sizes can you count in the picture?

....

TIME

FRACTIONAL PAIRS

Can you join all of the numbers below into pairs, so that each pair adds up to a total of 5?

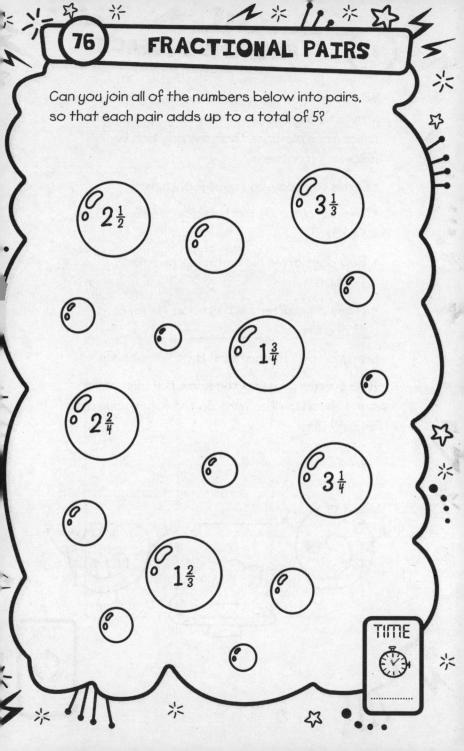

$2\frac{1}{2}$

$3\frac{1}{3}$

$1\frac{3}{4}$

$2\frac{2}{4}$

$3\frac{1}{4}$

$1\frac{2}{3}$

TIME

....

Will receives a new camera for his birthday, and starts taking pictures every day. Each day he takes more pictures than the day before, following a pattern:

- On his birthday, he takes 2 photos.

- The day after his birthday, he takes 5 photos.

- Two days after his birthday, he takes 11 photos.

- Three days after his birthday, he takes 23 photos.

Can you spot the pattern that Will is using?

If he carries on using the same pattern, how many photos will he take on the fourth day after his birthday?

....

TIME

....

SKILLS TEST

Test your mental arithmetic with these puzzles!

Begin with the number at the top of each puzzle and apply all of the instructions in turn, from top to bottom. Keep going until you reach the empty bottom box, then write your answer there.
To make it extra tricky, try to do all of the sums in your head, without writing anything down until each final answer.

In the first puzzle, for example, you would start with 8, then multiply by 2 (to make 16), then add 3 (to make 19) and so on.

8	20	7
×2	+4	+15
+3	÷12	÷11
×3	+6	+13
+10	×10	×3
-14	-9	-4

TIME
....

SUM DIFFERENCE

All of the sums that are in the same position on these two pictures have the same answer, apart from five. Can you circle the five sums whose answers are different?

9×10

60+5

11+22

100+50

7×5

10+15

99-98

6×2

4×5

11×5

7+7

25÷5

8×2

32÷4

55+44

Once you have found the five different sum results, can you also find five visual differences between the two pictures?

You have 27 blocks built into a 3x3x3 tower, so they look like this:

EXAMPLE:

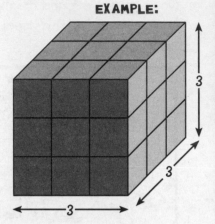

3
3
3

You build three more identical block towers, then take some blocks away from each tower. How many blocks are left in each pile now?

I.

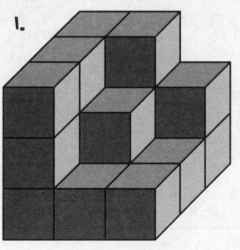

.... blocks left

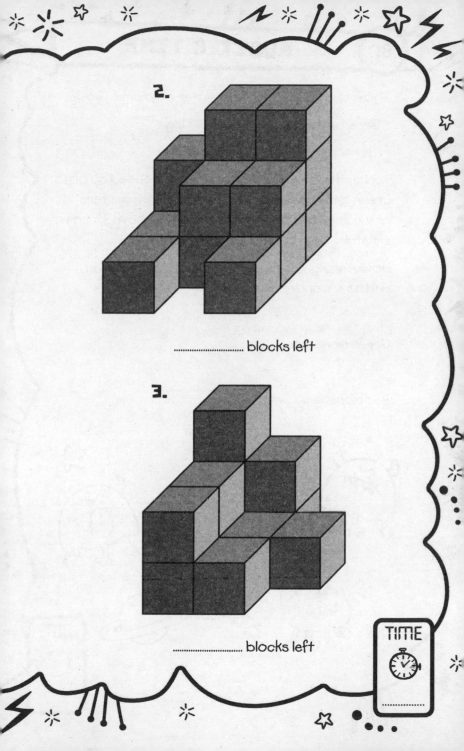

2.

.... blocks left

3.

.... blocks left

TIME

MONSTER TIME

There are two types of monster on planet Gloop:

- Green monsters, which have 3 legs.

- Red monsters, which have 4 legs.

Today there is a birthday that is attended by both green and red monsters. There are 12 monsters attending, and between them all they have 42 legs in total.

How many green monsters are at the birthday, and how many red monsters?

Green monsters ....

Red monsters ....

TIME

....

FAMILY TREE

Zara is writing out her family tree, and asks her grandmother for some help.

She asks her grandmother how many children she has. She replies, 'I have two sons, and each of those two sons has two sisters.'

Then, Zara asks her grandmother how many grandchildren she has. She replies, 'Neither of my sons has any children. Each of my daughters has two sons, and each of those two sons has one sister.'

1. How many children does Zara's grandmother have?

....

2. How many grandchildren does Zara's grandmother have?

....

TIME

....

Can you complete each of these puzzles by writing a number from 1 to 6 in every empty square? No number can repeat within any row or column.

Any squares which are joined by a shaded bar have a *difference* of 4.

This means that if you subtract the smaller number from the larger number, you end up with a result of 4.

Also, any squares which are *not* separated by a shaded bar **do not have a difference of 4.** You'll need to make use of this rule to solve the puzzle.

Here's an example solution to show how it works:

EXAMPLE:

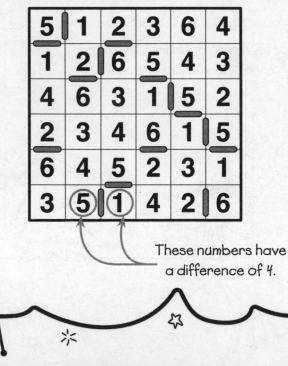

These numbers have a difference of 4.

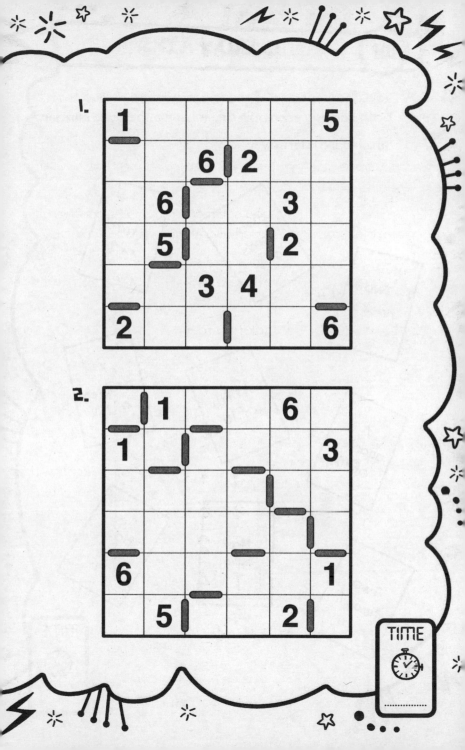

CARD PAIRS

Join all except one of these cards into pairs, so that both cards in each pair are equal to the same number.

Which card is left over?

Two-thirds of 6

A third of 9

Two times 5

A fifth of 10

A quarter of 16

A quarter of 40

Half of 6

Half of 28

Two times 7

TIME

POCKET MONEY

Carla and her parents live in Yosia, where the currency is the yakka. This is usually shortened to 'y', so it's easier to write.

This week, Carla is receiving pocket money from her parents every day.

• Today is Monday, and Carla is given 1y.

• Each day of the week from Tuesday onwards, her parents decide to increase the amount she receives by 2y. For example, on Tuesday this means she will receive 3y (which is 1y from the previous day, plus the 2y increase).

On what day of the week will Carla first be able to afford something that costs 25y? Assume that she had no money before the week began, and that she doesn't spend any of the money until she has saved up 25y.

ALL THE ANSWERS

NUMBER RIDDLE 1

11

NUMBER RIDDLE 2

Jenny is 12. Sam is 7. Miriam is 6.
We can work this out like this:

- Miriam is two years younger than Yaz was last week, when Yaz would have been 8, so Miriam is 6.

- Jenny is double Miriam's age, so her age is 2x6 = 12.

- Sam is one year older than Miriam, so she is 7.

NUMBER RIDDLE 3

There are 2 yellow monsters and 2 blue monsters.

The yellow monsters have 6 legs in total, since 2 x 3 = 6.

The blue monsters have 8 legs in total, since 2 x 4 = 8.

This fits with the overall total of 6 + 8 = 14 legs.

NUMBER RIDDLE 4

7 = 5 + 2

12 = 5 + 7

17 = 8 + 9

ANSWERS

NUMBER RIDDLE 5

1. 15 lengths.
   Each day Jaz swims
   3 more lengths than
   the previous day.

2. On Sunday she will
   swim 21 lengths.

NUMBER RIDDLE 6

They could pour 1 half-full
jar into the other half-full
jar. Then they will each be
able to take home 2 full
jars and 1 empty jar.

NUMBER RIDDLE 7

1. 4 blocks
2. 4 blocks
3. 5 blocks

NUMBER RIDDLE 8

- Roll 1 = 2
- Roll 2 = 5
- Roll 3 = 3
- Roll 4 = 4

NUMBER RIDDLE 9

1. You should finish at 7
   - Start at 3
   - Jump to 5
   - Jump to 10
   - Then jump to 7

2. You would need to
   add 4, since 3 (starting
   number) + 4 = 7
   (finishing number).

NUMBER RIDDLE 10

7 + 2   and   5 + 3

9 x 10   and   100 – 9

30 + 5   and   10 – 5

25 – 15   and   11 + 5

3 x 3   and   12 – 4

The five picture differences are circled below.

NUMBER RIDDLE 11

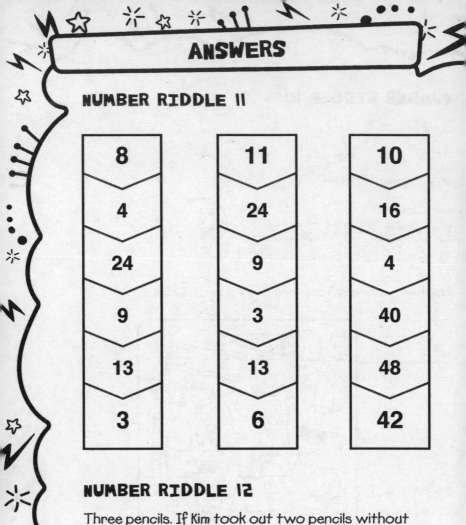

8	11	10
4	24	16
24	9	4
9	3	40
13	13	48
3	6	42

NUMBER RIDDLE 12

Three pencils. If Kim took out two pencils without looking, she might take one of each colour. But, when she takes out a third pencil, it must match at least one of the two she has already taken.

NUMBER RIDDLE 13

1. 7
2. 6

NUMBER RIDDLE 14

43 minutes. She will spend 8 minutes in total eating (8 x 1 = 8), and then 7 x 5 = 35 minutes waiting in between eating. Together, these times add up to 43 minutes, since 8 + 35 = 43.

NUMBER RIDDLE 15

31 is the odd number out, since it is the only one that is odd (that is, not divisible by 2 into another whole number).

NUMBER RIDDLE 16

- 5×1 pairs with $3 + 2 = 5$
- $4 + 2$ pairs with $12 \div 2 = 6$
- $7 - 4$ pairs with $9 \div 3 = 3$
- 2×5 pairs with $6 + 4 = 10$
- $9 - 1$ is the one left over $= 8$

NUMBER RIDDLE 17

1. The picture can be drawn using just 4 rectangles.

2. There are 8 different rectangles in the picture.

NUMBER RIDDLE 18

Person	Finishing position	Number of marshmallows
Nat	First	6
Sara	Second	3
Evan	Third	2

NUMBER RIDDLE 19

3 and 6	5 and 10
7 and 14	8 and 16
9 and 18	11 and 22

NUMBER RIDDLE 20

1. Balloons 4 + 12   2. Balloons 6 + 15

3. Balloons 4 + 8 + 12   4. Balloons 8 + 12 + 15

NUMBER RIDDLE 21

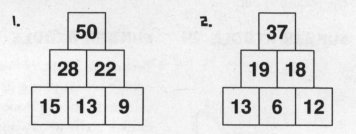

1.

	50	
28	22	
15	13	9

2.

	37	
19	18	
13	6	12

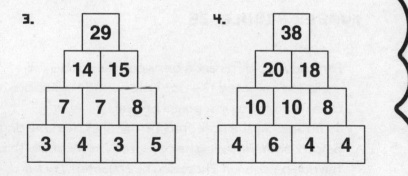

3.

	29		
14	15		
7	7	8	
3	4	3	5

4.

	38		
20	18		
10	10	8	
4	6	4	4

NUMBER RIDDLE 22

Julia can fill the four-unit cup to the top, then use this to fill the three-unit cup to the top. This will leave exactly one unit in the four-unit cup.

NUMBER RIDDLE 23

1. 7:00pm
2. 8:30pm
3. 5:00pm
4. 4:30am
5. 5:00pm

NUMBER RIDDLE 24

1. $12 = 5 + 7$
2. $18 = 8 + 10$
3. $20 = 9 + 11$

NUMBER RIDDLE 25

Two magic beans. At every bridge he will hand over one bean, then get one back – so he will always have two magic beans both before and after crossing every bridge.

NUMBER RIDDLE 26

1. 17 shells.
   Each day, the difference between the number of shells Jon collected the day before and the number he collects that day increases by one.
   So on Tuesday he collected 1 more shell than the day before; on Wednesday he collected 2 more shells than the day before; on Thursday he collected 3 more shells than the day before; and so on.

2. On Sunday he will collect 23 shells.

NUMBER RIDDLE 27

12

The item prices after discount are:

NUMBER RIDDLE 28

7

NUMBER RIDDLE 29

- 45+5 = 50
- 30+50 = 80
- 32÷4 = 8
- 13x2 = 26
- 100÷10 = 10
- 8x3 = 24

NUMBER RIDDLE 30

1.

2	4	5	3	1
1	3	2	4	5
4	5	3	1	2
5	1	4	2	3
3	2	1	5	4

2.

2	1	3	4	5
4	2	1	5	3
5	4	2	3	1
3	5	4	1	2
1	3	5	2	4

NUMBER RIDDLE 31

1. 12
2. 10

NUMBER RIDDLE 32

NUMBER RIDDLE 33

There are four brothers and three sisters. This means that Amos has three brothers and three sisters, and Zoe has four brothers and two sisters.

NUMBER RIDDLE 34

1. We are told Doug eats 4 slices of pizza.
   Fai must eat 1 slice of pizza, since a quarter of 4 is 1.
   Nic must eat 3 slices of pizza, because a quarter of 12 is 3.

2. There are 4 pieces of pizza left. The friends ate 8 pieces in total, and 12 − 8 = 4.

3. $\frac{2}{3}$ of the original pizza has been eaten. This is the same as $\frac{8}{12}$, so if you wrote that down then that's correct, too.

NUMBER RIDDLE 35

1.

	27	
17		10
12	5	5

2.

	25	
12		13
6	6	7

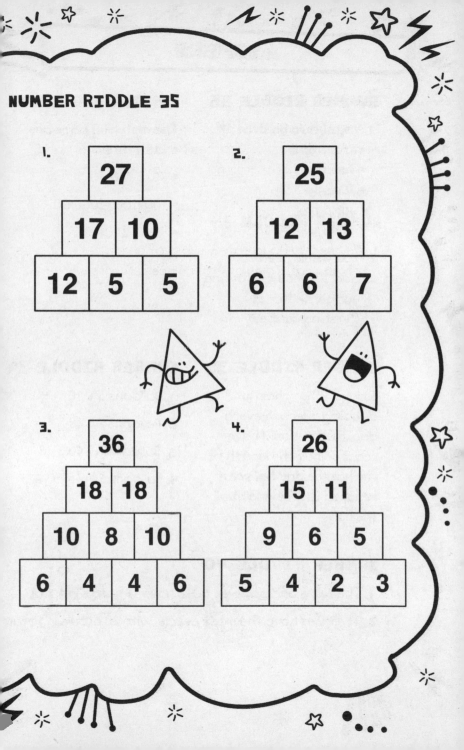

3.

	36		
18		18	
10	8	10	
6	4	4	6

4.

	26		
15		11	
9	6	5	
5	4	2	3

ANSWERS

NUMBER RIDDLE 36

1. You should finish at 14:
   - Start at 4
   - Jump to 1
   - Jump to 9
   - Jump to 7
   - Then jump to 14

2. You would need to add 10, since 4 (starting number) + 10 = 14 (finishing number).

NUMBER RIDDLE 37

The matching pairs are:
- 1x5   20÷4
- 30x2   80-20
- 100x100   1000x10
- 55x2   100+10
- 35÷5   14÷2

NUMBER RIDDLE 38

5 days. If her chain is doubling in length every day, then it would have reached half the length of the hall the day *before* it reached the full length of the hall.

NUMBER RIDDLE 39

1. Balloons 5 + 10
2. Balloons 7 + 13
3. Balloons 7 + 10 + 13
4. Balloons 5 + 7 + 10 + 14

NUMBER RIDDLE 40

1. The tulips and poppies both have 18 petals in total.

2. The irises have the most petals, with 30 petals in total.

NUMBER RIDDLE 41

Option d: Luci will eat 16 grapes and Dan will eat 11. Each day Luci eats two **times** as many grapes as the day before, and Dan eats two **more** grapes than the day before.

NUMBER RIDDLE 42

1. $9 = 3 + 5 + 1$ **2.** $28 = 9 + 11 + 8$ **3.** $35 = 12 + 13 + 10$

NUMBER RIDDLE 43

1. 8th April. On the 8th he will have made 4 hats, on the 9th he will complete the 8th hat, on the 10th he will complete the 12th hat, and on the 11th the 16th hat.

2. 11th April, the day of the party. Eddie will have made 2 hats on the 8th, 4 hats by the end of the 9th, 6 hats by the end of the 10th, and 8 hats by the end of the 11th. 8 hats is half of the 16 hats he needs.

NUMBER RIDDLE 44

1. The picture can be drawn using just 5 rectangles.

2. There are 25 different rectangles in the picture.

ANSWERS

NUMBER RIDDLE 45

She can separate each pair into two socks, and give one sock from each pair to her and to Ron. They will both receive the same selection of socks, and because there are two pairs of each colour they will both receive two of each colour.

NUMBER RIDDLE 46

Julia should fill the 3-unit cup to the top and pour it into the 4-unit cup. Then she should fill the 3-unit cup to the top again and pour as much as she can into the 4-unit cup, until it is full. This will then leave exactly 2 units in the 3-unit cup.

NUMBER RIDDLE 47

2 and 8	3 and 12
5 and 20	7 and 28
9 and 36	10 and 40

NUMBER RIDDLE 48

1. 11 blocks
2. 9 blocks
3. 7 blocks

NUMBER RIDDLE 49

1. 16   2. 18

NUMBER RIDDLE 50

1. 7:00

2. 7:30

3. 12:00

4. 1:15

5. 12:15

NUMBER RIDDLE 51

1.

5	1	4	3	2
2	4	1	5	3
4	5	3	2	1
3	2	5	1	4
1	3	2	4	5

2.

4	3	2	5	1
3	1	5	2	4
5	4	1	3	2
2	5	4	1	3
1	2	3	4	5

ANSWERS

NUMBER RIDDLE 52

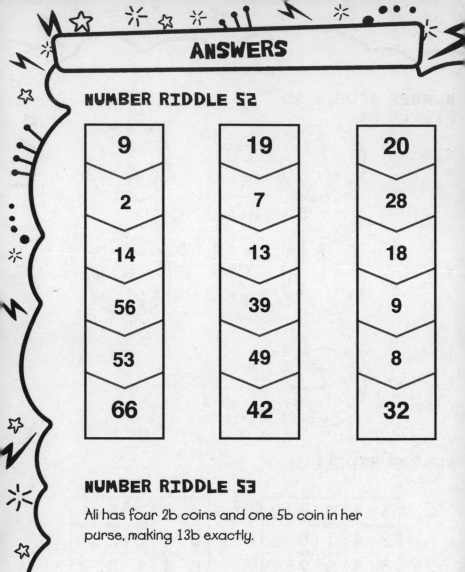

9	19	20
2	7	28
14	13	18
56	39	9
53	49	8
66	42	32

NUMBER RIDDLE 53

Ali has four 2b coins and one 5b coin in her purse, making 13b exactly.

NUMBER RIDDLE 54

1.

		54		
	26	28		
	12	14	14	
5	7	7	7	
1	4	3	4	3

2.

		57		
	29	28		
	16	13	15	
9	7	6	9	
4	5	2	4	5

3.

		62		
	31	31		
	14	17	14	
5	9	8	6	
1	4	5	3	3

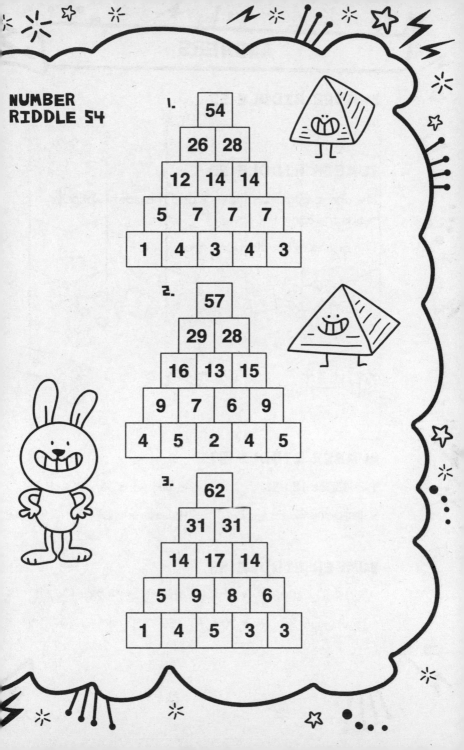

ANSWERS

NUMBER RIDDLE 55

4

NUMBER RIDDLE 56

The cheapest item is the dice and the most expensive item is the car.

The prices after discount are:

NUMBER RIDDLE 57

1. Balloons 12 + 13
2. Balloons 13 + 20
3. Balloons 12 + 18 + 19
4. Balloons 12 + 13 + 19 + 20

NUMBER RIDDLE 58

- 100 x 10 = 1000
- 50 ÷ 5 = 10
- 28 ÷ 4 = 7
- 15 x 2 = 30
- 20 + 40 = 60
- 14 + 90 = 104

NUMBER RIDDLE 59

1. Saturday will be the first day that Stephen mends over 20 socks in a single day. He will mend 16 socks on Friday, but 32 on Saturday.

2. Stephen will have more than 50 socks in his drawer on Saturday, since he will have exactly 63 socks in the drawer at the end of the day.

Here are the totals for Monday to Saturday:

Monday	1 sock mended	1 sock in the drawer
Tuesday	2 socks mended	3 socks in the drawer
Wednesday	4 socks mended	7 socks in the drawer
Thursday	8 socks mended	15 socks in the drawer
Friday	16 socks mended	31 socks in the drawer
Saturday	32 socks mended	63 socks in the drawer

NUMBER RIDDLE 60

Option a: Ava will paint 6 pictures and Sophie will paint 1. Each week, Ava paints **11 fewer** pictures than the week before, and Sophie paints **a third** of the number of pictures as the week before – which means that the number she painted last week is divided by three.

ANSWERS

NUMBER RIDDLE 61

1. There are 8 layers in the pyramid.

2. There are 36 blocks in the top 3 layers of the pyramid: 6 + 12 + 18 = 36.

NUMBER RIDDLE 62

1. 21 = 4 + 12 + 5

2. 30 = 4 + 12 + 14

3. 35 = 11 + 10 + 14

NUMBER RIDDLE 63

Four pencils.
In the worst case, the first three pencils might all be the same colour. The fourth pencil, however, must then be a different colour.

NUMBER RIDDLE 64

1. There are 9 yellow sweets, as the first clue states.
There are 12 pink sweets, since 24 ÷ 2 = 12. There are 3 red sweets, since 24 − 9 (yellow) − 12 (pink) = 3.

2. Each person would get 4 pink sweets, since 12 (pink sweets) ÷ 3 (the number of people) = 4

3. Yes. They would get 4 pink sweets (as per answer 2), 3 yellow sweets and 1 red sweet.

NUMBER RIDDLE 65

1. 10. Each of the people will be given 1 brownie, 2 muffins, 3 cookies and 4 cupcakes.

2. 1. There were 3 brownies and 2 chocolate-chip cookies left over, before you ate 4 of them.

NUMBER RIDDLE 66

9

NUMBER RIDDLE 67

Rob is looking at a clock.

On a normal 12-hour clock face, moving 10 around the clock face will bring you from 7 o'clock to 5 o'clock. Adding 4 to a clock showing 9 o'clock would bring you to 1 o'clock, and adding 5 to a clock showing 11 o'clock would bring you to 4 o'clock.

NUMBER RIDDLE 68

The matching pairs are:

- 3x6 = 9x2
- 36÷4 = 18÷2
- 101x2 = 300-98
- 250x4 = 1000x1
- 17+17 = 40-6

ANSWERS

NUMBER
RIDDLE 69

1.

80

| 20 | 4 |

| 5 | 4 | 1 |

2.

20

| 5 | 4 |

| 5 | 1 | 4 |

3.

60

| 6 | 10 |

| 3 | 2 | 5 |

NUMBER RIDDLE 70

Freddy and Mia could break all five loops on one chain, then use those to connect the remaining five chains together.

NUMBER RIDDLE 71

1. Balloons 8 + 9
2. Balloons 6 + 15
3. Balloons 6 + 8 + 14
4. Balloons 6 + 14 + 15

NUMBER RIDDLE 72

1. February. It is the only month which can be made of an exact number of weeks, when it isn't a leap year – so it's the only month which can start on a Monday and end on a Sunday.

2. July and August. They are the only two months in the year with exactly 31 days which follow one after the other, to give the total of 62 days.

NUMBER RIDDLE 73

Aunt Vicki. We can work this out like this:

• Aunty Kathleen's donation will be £12 for the first 5 miles, plus 5 x £4 = £20 for the remaining 5 miles, which makes £32 in total.

• Aunty Vicki's donation will be £10 for the first 2 miles, plus 8 x £3 = £24 for the remaining 8 miles left, which makes £34 in total.

ANSWERS

NUMBER RIDDLE 74

1. 21

2. 6

NUMBER RIDDLE 75

1. There are 14 squares: 9 of the smallest size (1x1), 4 of the middle size (2x2), and 1 of the largest size (3x3).

2. There are 22 rectangles, not including squares: 6 2x1 rectangles, 6 1x2 rectangles, 3 3x1 rectangles, 3 1x3 rectangles, 2 3x2 rectangles and 2 2x3 rectangles.

NUMBER RIDDLE 76

$1\frac{3}{4}$ + $3\frac{1}{4}$ = 5

$2\frac{1}{2}$ + $2\frac{2}{4}$ = 5

$3\frac{1}{3}$ + $1\frac{2}{3}$ = 5

NUMBER RIDDLE 77

47.
Each day Will takes two times as many photos as the day before, plus one more. (This is the same as saying that the **increase** in the number of photos he takes doubles each day).

NUMBER RIDDLE 78

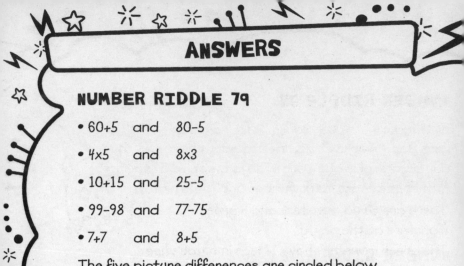

ANSWERS

NUMBER RIDDLE 79

- 60+5 and 80-5
- 4x5 and 8x3
- 10+15 and 25-5
- 99-98 and 77-75
- 7+7 and 8+5

The five picture differences are circled below.

NUMBER RIDDLE 80

1. 19 blocks　　**2.** 15 blocks　　**3.** 12 blocks

NUMBER RIDDLE 81

There are 6 red monsters and 6 green monsters at the party.
The green monsters have 18 legs in total, since $6 \times 3 = 18$. The red monsters have 24 legs in total, since $6 \times 4 = 24$. This fits with the overall total of $18 + 24 = 42$ legs.

NUMBER RIDDLE 82

1. Zara's grandmother has 4 children: 2 sons and 2 daughters. Although both sons have 2 sisters, they are the same 2 sisters.

2. Zara's grandmother has 6 grandchildren: 4 grandsons and 2 granddaughters. Each of her 2 daughters has 2 sons – these are the 4 grandsons. Each of those 4 grandsons has 1 sister, but for each pair of grandsons these are the same sister – so there are 2 granddaughters.

NUMBER RIDDLE 83

1.

1	2	4	3	6	5
5	4	6	2	1	3
4	6	2	5	3	1
3	5	1	6	2	4
6	1	3	4	5	2
2	3	5	1	4	6

2.

5	1	2	3	6	4
1	2	6	5	4	3
4	6	3	1	5	2
2	3	4	6	1	5
6	4	5	2	3	1
3	5	1	4	2	6

NUMBER RIDDLE 84

- Half of 6 pairs with a third of 9 = 3
- Two times 7 pairs with half of 28 = 14
- A quarter of 16 pairs with two-thirds of 6 = 4
- A quarter of 40 pairs with two times 5 = 10
- A fifth of 10 is the odd card out = 2

NUMBER RIDDLE 85

Friday. It will take Carla five days to save up 25y. Here is how much money she has on each day:

- Monday – Carla receives 1y, for 1y total.
- Tuesday – Carla receives 3y, for 4y total.
- Wednesday – Carla receives 5y, for 9y total.
- Thursday – Carla receives 7y, for 16y total.
- Friday – Carla receives 9y, for 25y total.

NOTES AND SCRIBBLES

NOTES

NOTES

NOTES

NOTES

NOTES

NOTES

NOTES

NOTES

NOTES

ALSO AVAILABLE:

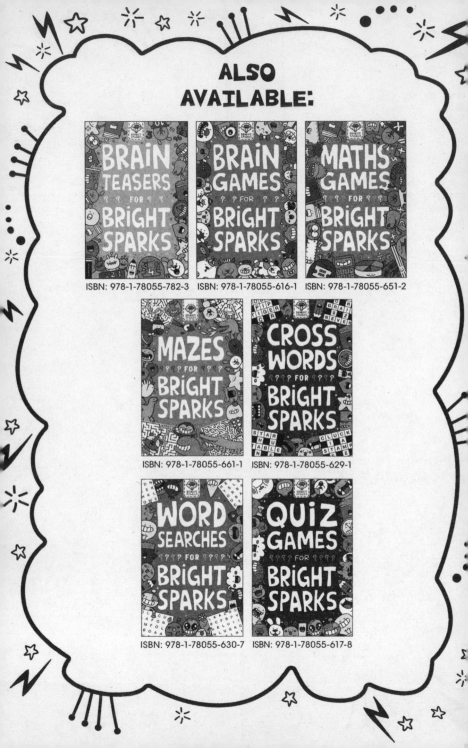